920 S
Spada: Captain and Tennille

180847

DISCARD

Norwich Middle School
Library Media Center
Norwich, N.Y.

Norwich Middle School
Library Media Center
Norwich, N.Y.

Captain &
Tennille

by James Spada
designed by Mark Landkamer

CREATIVE EDUCATION
CHILDRENS PRESS

Published by Creative Education, Inc., 123 South Broad Street, Mankato, Minnesota 56001 Copyright © 1978 by Creative Education, Inc. International copyrights reserved in all countries. No part of this book may be reproduced in any form without written permission from the publisher. Printed in the United States.

Library of Congress Cataloging in Publication Data

Spada, James.
   Captain and Tennille.

   SUMMARY: Describes the marriage and career of a popular singing duo.
   1. Captain and Tennille—Juvenile literature. 2. Rock musicians—United States—Biography—Juvenile literature. [1. Captain and Tennille. 2. Musicians]
I. Title.
ML3930.C25S7   784'.092'2 [B] [92] 77-24625
ISBN 0-87191-615-0

Photographs:

A&M Records	9, 16, 22, 26
Globe Photos/Nate Cutler	cover

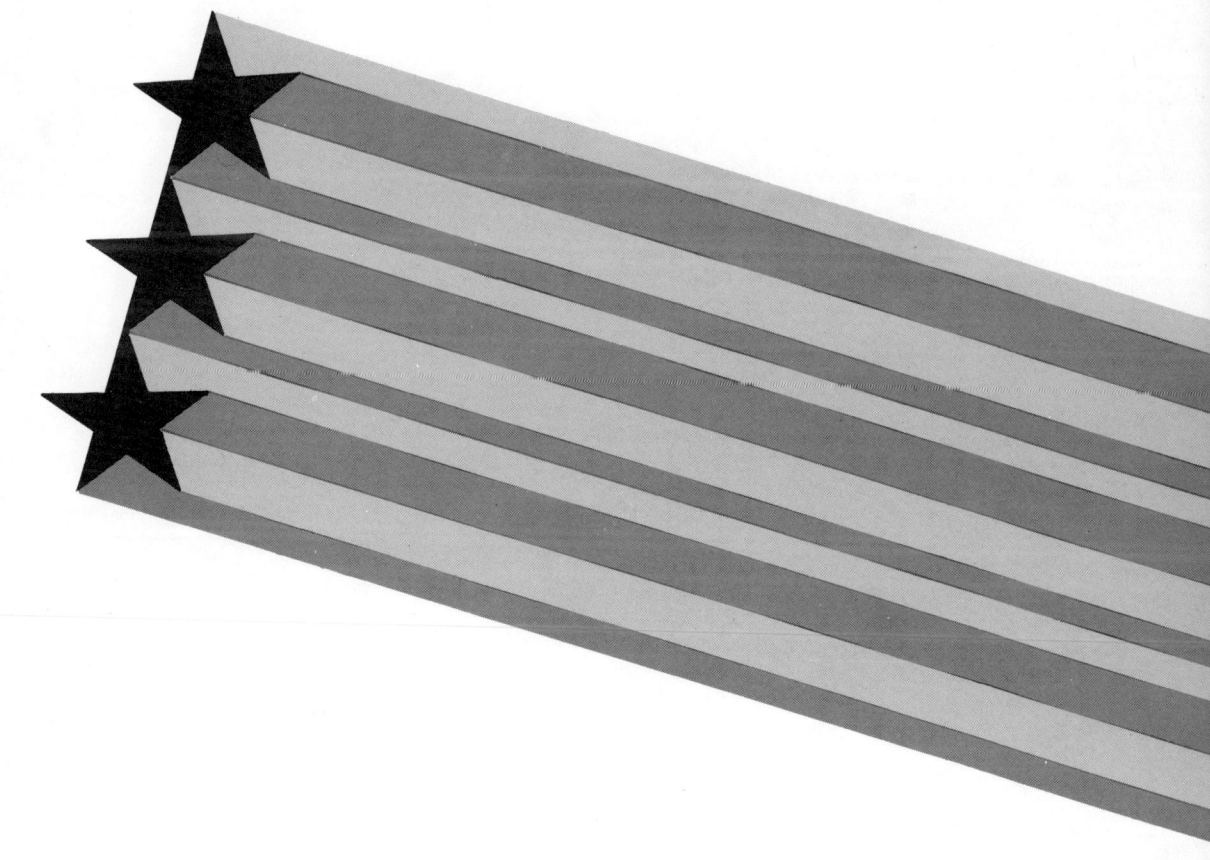

Love Will Keep Us Together

Every week, millions of Americans turn on their TV sets to watch them. Their first five records have all gone Gold, meaning that they have sold at least one million copies each. Across the country, people flock to their concerts, paying from five to 25 dollars to hear them perform.

You don't have to be a genius to figure out that the Captain and Tennille are one of the most popular singing duos around today. Their success has come quickly and in such large doses that neither of them can believe it, even now. And yet, they always knew they'd make it—even during the lean years when nobody seemed interested in them and they had to spend their own money to bring their music to the people. What made them so sure? The fact that they were so much in love. They knew whatever happened to them, they'd see things through on the sheer strength of their devotion to each other.

But, even more importantly, love has played a large part in their popularity, too. Their first record success was "The Way I Want To Touch You," a song that Toni Tennille wrote about her husband, the Captain. And TV viewers really enjoy watching the couple, because their affection for each other is so obvious.

Tonie Tennille and Daryl Dragon (that's the Captain's real name) are two people who are as different as night and day. Toni is energetic, animated, talkative, upbeat and has a dazzling smile to rival President Carter's. Her husband, on the other hand, is quiet, shy, low-key, careful and deliberate in his speech and movement. He doesn't say much at all, usually leaving the talking to Toni. At first it seems that they would have very little in common. But the reason they get along so well is that they both have a very deep love of music. And it was music that brought them together in the first place.

Flashback – Toni

Toni and Daryl didn't meet until they were in their late twenties. Toni was born on May 8 and she was raised in Montgomery, Alabama. She was named Cathryn Antoinette, after her mom, and the family gave her the nickname Toni. She has three sisters, Jane, Louisa and Melissa. The four girls couldn't help but become interested in music, because their father, Frank Tennille, had been a singer with several big bands in the 1930's. Their mother was the hostess of a local TV show, and Toni and her sisters would hang around the studio whenever they could. Toni was taking lessons in classical piano then, and every so often her mother would let her play the piano for the exercise lady who appeared on the program. Toni also studied dancing and singing, and once in a while she got a chance to dance or sing with her sisters on Mom's show.

Toni loved performing but sometimes she would get tired of studying and practicing piano and want to give it up. But she stuck to it, with some firm encouragement from her mother and father. Now, she says, "All the voice lessons, dance lessons and theatre arts work was worth it. It all came together when the public starting paying attention to us."

In school, Toni did well and she liked to participate in class discussions. "I was always the girl in the front row raising her hand and wanting to be called on," she remembers. When she graduated from high school, Toni decided to go to college at Auburn University. While she was there she studied music and was the lead singer with a popular campus band. By now, Toni had decided that music was going to be her life.

During her second year at college, Toni's father decided to move the family to California when his furniture business failed. Toni's mom was reluctant to give up her TV show which had been running for five years. "But being a good wife, she went with Dad and gave up the show," says Toni. "She's always regretted it and they were divorced soon afterward." Toni was quite upset when her parents broke up, but she vowed to remain close to both of them and did so. She was soon to know the heartache of divorce for herself.

At her college, Toni says, everyone thought that if you weren't married by 22 you were an "old maid." She knows now how silly that kind of thinking was, but at the time she took it seriously. She decided to get married before really thinking about it, and it wasn't long before she was sorry. The man she married, a rock drummer named Kenneth Shearer, "is and was a lovely man," she says. "But we both knew it was wrong almost from the first." They were divorced not too long after their wedding. Now, Toni believes one of the songs she sings really has an important message. "I didn't 'shop around.' That's why I sing that song with feeling now."

Eventually, Toni moved to California too, to be closer to her parents and sisters. She got a job as a file clerk and wrote music whenever she had the chance. It wasn't long before she would meet the man who would mean more to her than anyone else.

Flashback – The Captain

Like Toni, young Daryl Dragon had a family background rich in music. His father, Carmen Dragon, is a well-known symphony conductor who for years conducted the Hollywood Bowl Symphony and has recorded many record albums. Daryl was born August 27. Growing up in Los Angeles with two brothers and two sisters, Daryl was encouraged by his dad to study classical piano. At first, he resisted. "You know how you are when you're little," says Daryl. "I said, 'I'm not going to go into music.' " But when his dad introduced him to it, Daryl really liked it. And having such a talented, accomplished father helped Daryl succeed at his studies. "When I got stuck with a music problem, I'd bring it home and ask him to help me. I felt a little guilty about it because the other kids couldn't do that."

Daryl became very wrapped up in his music. It was a way in which he could express himself. He was always very shy and quiet, feeling as though he couldn't keep up with his brothers. "My older brother Doug was lively and outgoing," Daryl remembers, "and my younger brother Dennis was always up. So I decided the best thing to do was lay back."

But Daryl was so quiet and retiring that people started to worry about him. When he was in school in Santa Monica, California, the principal called his parents and told them, "Your son is disturbed." The principal wanted to put Daryl in an institution to help him with his emotional problems. "But it wasn't anything more than just being shy," says Daryl. A year later he was chosen as a Boy of the Month by the Elks Club. Daryl was able to prove that even quiet, shy youngsters can be good students, and contribute something. "They picked me out of all the kids in my class," Daryl says with pride. "Now I look back and say, 'Boy, were they right!' "

In college at California State University at Northridge, Daryl continued his traditional training, studying organ and learning to play every kind of keyboard instrument ever made—plus the electronic synthesizer, vibes and electronic bass. But after a while he got tired of classical music and decided to do something about his love of Fats Domino and the Blues. So he and brothers Doug and Dennis formed a boogie-woogie group called The Dragons. They recorded an album for Capitol Records, the same company that had released their dad's symphony albums. The album was not successful. Daryl thinks it was because just at that time the Beatles were becoming popular. "We were an instrumental group and you had to sing in those days." Also, rock 'n' roll was changing then. Heavy rock and the drug culture were becoming popular. That wasn't the kind of music Daryl and his brothers liked to play. "I couldn't relate to dope groups," says Daryl, "and I was afraid of destroying my ears with loud sound."

Daryl and his brothers pursued separate careers, and soon Daryl was playing keyboard for the Beach

Boys. He didn't do this all the time; just when they needed him. It was during one of the times he wasn't playing with the group that he met Toni Tennille.

The World's Only Beachgirl

It didn't take too long for Toni to get tired of being a file clerk, so she joined the South Coast Repertory Theatre, playing various parts and helping out with all phases of backstage work. But what Toni really wanted to do was write music. So she and a friend from the Repertory Company decided to write a musical for the group. Toni was able to combine her interest in music with her concern for the environment, and the show, called Mother Earth, had an ecological theme. It ran in San Francisco and got good reviews, then it moved on to Los Angeles. But the show's keyboard man couldn't leave San Francisco, so the company had to look for someone new. One of the cast members recommended Daryl Dragon, and he joined the group.

Daryl liked the music that Toni had written. She was glad, because she soon realized, she says, that "Daryl can't work with anybody whose music he doesn't respect." Toni also realized right away that Daryl was somebody special. "I'm more romantic than he is. I was struck by him the first day we met. But he just sat there silently listening to the music. Even though he didn't say a word, I told myself, 'There's something here.'"

Toni soon found out that Daryl liked her, too, because after Mother Earth stopped playing he recommended her as a keyboard player for the Beach

Boys. She joined the group and went on tour with them. She even sang backup a couple of times. To this day, Toni Tennille is the world's first—and only—Beach Girl.

Daryl's nickname, The Captain, came from the Beach Boys, too. One day he decided to wear a Captain's cap to go along with the surfing image of the Beach Boys. So Mike Love, leader of the group, started calling him "Captain Keyboard." The name got shortened to just "Captain," but it has stuck with Daryl ever since.

Trying for Success — Against the Odds

After touring for awhile with the Beach Boys, Toni and Daryl found themselves falling in love. Daryl suggested that they get married and form a singing duo. Toni said yes to both ideas. They were wed on Valentine's Day and set up housekeeping in a tiny stucco bungalow in California's San Fernando Valley. Their marriage got off to a much better start than their career as an act. For several years they worked in small clubs, mostly in Southern California. Sometimes they worked in five or six different clubs a week. It was a tough pace to keep up, but they never got discouraged. Not even when no one was interested in recording a song Toni had written about her love for the Captain.

The song was called "The Way I Want To Touch You," and it had a lovely melody and romantic lyrics. But hard as they tried, The Captain and Tennille couldn't convince a major recording studio to release it. Rather

than give up, though, they decided to make the record themselves. So one day they walked into a recording studio and paid 250 dollars to make 500 copies of the song. Daryl played all the instruments, and Toni sang all the vocals.

Once they had the record made, they brought it around to local radio stations and begged them to play it. Several disc jockeys, who were fans of the pair after seeing them at local clubs, agreed to play the record. It was an instant hit. The 500 copies were sold within several days. The demand for the record was so great that finally a major company, A&M Records, signed the duo and released the record on its own label. It was a top-ten hit on the West Coast, but it didn't become a national best-seller.

The Big Break

One day, while Toni and Daryl were looking for a new song to record for A&M, the company's vice-president suggested they listen to Neil Sedaka's new album. There was a great song on it, he said, that Sedaka wasn't planning to release as a single. The couple listened to the song, "Love Will Keep Us Together," and instantly agreed that it was just the kind of song they wanted to do — a good, upbeat, rock 'n' roll sound with lyrics that meant something to them.

The record was a smash. It sold two and a half million copies and was Number One on record charts across the country. Then the Captain and Tennille recorded an album, called "Love Will Keep Us

Together," and that recording sold over a million copies. After the success of their first single and the album, A&M records decided to re-release "The Way I Want To Touch You" nationally. That, too, became a Number One best-seller. Everything was coming together for the Captain and Tennille. And all this had happened within one year. It was an overnight success story, magazines and newspapers were saying. Yes, their success had happened quickly. But the Captain and Tennille knew it had truly come after years of hard work and sometimes discouragement. And that made the success all the sweeter when it did come.

"And the Winner Is..."

Early in 1975, Toni and Daryl discovered that they had been nominated for two Grammy Awards. The Grammies are the most coveted recognition recording artists can achieve, and neither of them thought they'd win. They had been nominated for Best Vocal Performance by a Group and for Song of the Year. Both nominations were for "Love Will Keep Us Together."

The Grammy Awards ceremony was a big event for both Toni and Daryl's families. "We bought so many Grammy tickets, they thought we were a record company," says Toni. It was the biggest night the family had ever had, and everyone got dressed up and they rented limousines to take everyone from their houses to the affair.

Before the show started, the Best Vocal Performance by a Group award had gone to the Eagles for "Lyin' Eyes." Toni and Daryl were disappointed, and they decided that they didn't have a chance to win Song of the Year. Toni remembers, " 'Lyin' Eyes' was competing against us for that award, too, so we weren't optimistic. Then after Janis Ian sang 'At 17' we were sure she would get it. Then Daryl decided it would be Barry Manilow for 'Mandy.' "

Toni and Daryl could hardly sit still until the time came for the winner's name to be announced. They were on pins and needles. Then Stevie Wonder called out their names as winners of the Song of the Year Award. "I must have come eight inches off the seat," says Toni. "We went up there and when I turned around and everybody was standing and applauding, I couldn't believe it. I cried."

The Captain and Tennille had received the acclaim of their colleagues in addition to the acceptance of the public. Their success was total and complete. And there would be more of it.

Personally Speaking

The Captain and Tennille were very happy. Professionally, they couldn't be more successful. And their personal life together couldn't be happier. The love they had for each other only grew as their success and popularity grew. The financial rewards of stardom allowed them to move from their tiny bungalow into a 7,000 square-foot English manor on top of California's Pacific Palisades, right at the ocean. The house has a

walk-in fireplace, avocado trees, an organic garden and paddle tennis court.

As beautiful as their house is, it wouldn't be quite as nice if it didn't have so much love. Toni and Daryl even wrote a song about their home. They call it "Butterscotch Castle" where "underneath the roof there are joy and love to share."

Also underneath the Captain and Tennille's roof are Elizabeth and Broderick, their sad-sack bulldogs. The dogs are members of the family, and they appear with their "parents" on album covers and every week on TV. The dogs receive almost as much fan mail as the Captain and Tennille do. Neither one of them has had any musical training, but The Captain insists they are fans of his music.

The Captain keeps a full set of drums in the bathroom, and his nautical caps in the bedroom. He has seventeen so far, and adds two a week. He doesn't have any plans at the moment to stop collecting the hats—no matter how much room they take up.

Staying Healthy

Both the Captain and Tennille are "ovo-lacto" vegetarians. That means that they eat no meat, only vegetable, fruits, eggs and dairy products. Daryl decided to become a vegetarian a couple of years ago when his doctor told him he had uric acid in his blood. The doctor warned him that this could cause high blood pressure and gout. One day soon after, he read a book of his father's on health foods and started

changing his diet. A year later, he went back to the doctor, who told him his blood was fine. "So I've been on health food ever since," he says.

Toni had never eaten much meat, and when she met Daryl she decided to become totally vegetarian. Since that time she has lost 22 pounds, slimming down from 160 lbs. to 138 lbs. The first thing Toni gave up on her new diet was white bread. She feels that whole wheat bread is much better. She also gave up white sugar and replaced it with natural honey or date sugar (made from finely ground dates).

A typical day's food for the Captain and Tennille consists of: Breakfast: one piece of plain whole-wheat bread, one poached egg, a half papaya sprinkled with date sugar. Lunch: a large raw-vegetable salad topped with sesame and sunflower seeds and a nonpreservative oil-and-cider-vinegar dressing. Dinner: large vegetable salad, natural cheeses and a side order of cooked vegetables.

While the couple is on tour, though, it is often hard to stick to their special diet. So they carry their own food supply with them. They have a huge trunk filled with a cooker, utensils, Granola, nuts, seed, honey, exotic fruits and vegetables, raisins and brown rice, and they take it with them wherever they go. According to the Captain, even dog Broderick is a vegetarian. "His favorite food is bananas."

Hitting the Bigtime on TV

The very first time the Captain and Tennille appeared on television, they were extremely nervous. It was Dick Clark's "American Bandstand," a show that is watched by millions of young people. Before that, Toni and Daryl had sung only before small groups, most of them around 200 or so, or at concerts of several thousands. But nothing like this. And they were both very grateful to Dick Clark for giving them such a big break on TV. Their song, "Love Will Keep Us Together," was only number 60 on the charts at that time, so Dick Clark was taking a chance putting them on TV. "But he kinda liked the song," says Toni, "so he gave us the chance."

The appearance was very successful, and Toni and Daryl kept getting more and more offers to be on different shows as their record kept climbing the charts until it was number one. The Captain and Tennille were lucky because a lot of different kinds of television shows could use them. "Like, we could do a 'Dinah' one day, then turn around and do a 'Don Kirshner's Rock Concert' the next day and be sort of believable in both situations," says Toni.

The reason for this was that the Captain and Tennille appealed to many people—young, old, fans of rock, fans of popular music, and even some people who don't like music too much at all. The duo began getting fan mail from viewers of the various shows they were on, and it became obvious to the top executives at CBS, NBC and ABC that they were popular enough to do a show of their own. When they first were asked it they wanted to do a show, they practically jumped up and down with excitement. It was something they both, especially Toni, had wanted to do for a long time. Toni says, "Just when 'Love Will Keep Us Together' starting climbing up the charts, my manager asked me what I wanted to do with my career. I told him, almost a year before we signed the contract to do our show, that I wanted to have my own TV show." The Captain adds, "Toni has wanted to be on TV since I met her, ever since she was on TV with her mother in Alabama."

Because all three major networks wanted to sign them up, the Captain and Tennille were in the unusual position of being able to pick and choose. Toni explains why they decided on ABC: "We felt CBS was just too big and they didn't really understand what we were. NBC wanted to put us in a comedy like 'The Partridge Family.' We went 'Oh no!' But ABC seemed to understand what Daryl and I wanted to do."

It was important to the Captain and Tennille that they be allowed to be themselves on their TV show. "We can't pretend to be something we're not," says Toni. "I can't pretend to be sophisticated and I'm not a glamor girl with sophisticated hair-dos." They were glad that ABC didn't try to change the Captain, either. "Daryl's not going to go on TV and talk all the time," says Toni. "ABC realized that although Daryl's humor is a little strange, it could still be really funny."

So they decided to make the show like they would a home movie—with Toni just being her happy, talkative, bouncy, funny self and Daryl being his quiet, deadpan, shy, funny self. They brought their bulldogs, Broderick and Elizabeth, into the act, too—they introduce the show every week. And just to make sure it really is a family affair, Toni's sisters sing back-up and Daryl's brother Dennis plays the drums. Their families are very important to the Captain and Tennille.

There were many problems Toni and Daryl had to face when they first showed up for rehearsals at the TV studio. Everything was so new to them. "It was really tough learning to read cue cards and having to stand in a certain spot all the time," says The Captain. "And everything on TV is done so quickly. There isn't much time for rehearsals or re-takes, like in the movies. When you're on TV, you have to be good, and fast."

Another problem for the pair was that there were many things they wanted to do but couldn't. "We wanted to have guests who weren't what you'd call TV draws, fabulous people like Phoebe Snow, Randy Newman, Maria Muldaur. But ABC wanted people with proven drawing power like Bob Hope and Art Carney, just to make sure the show would get a big audience." Toni and Daryl hope that soon they'll be able to have some lesser-known, but no less talented and enjoyable, guests.

And it looks like they will be able to, because their show is a big success. It is one of the highest-rated shows on TV now. Audiences that watch their show, just like the people who buy their records or go to their concerts, really enjoy the Captain and Tennille. It's so obvious that they're having fun on their show that it's almost impossible not to have fun with them. And their music is so good. When all the clowning is over, The Captain sits down at the keyboard and plays as well as anyone. And Tennille can sing a song with the best of them. The show is great fun also because Toni and Daryl kid themselves and each other. But it's good-natured ribbing. "I won't make fun of Daryl like Cher does with Sonny," says Toni. "I refuse to do that. I don't do that in real life and I'm not going to do it on television. He makes fun of himself with his hat jokes, but we don't ever put each other down, no way, because that's not real if we do that."

Smile for Me One More Time

Happiness is a very important thing to the Captain and Tennille. They are happy, joyful, full of love. Their music reflects that: "Song Of Joy," "Muskrat Love," "Butterscotch Castle." In one song Toni Tennille wrote, she tries to cheer the Captain up because he'd gotten sad about something:

"And what you and me gotta do is / We gotta chase that old cloud away."

Some people make fun of the Captain and Tennille or criticize them. The Captain, they say, is too deadpan and doesn't talk enough. Tennille, they think, is too happy-go-lucky. "I really don't know what these people expect," says Toni. "All Daryl and I do is what is honest to us. We have to express ourselves. And wouldn't it be awful if we were both like me? We'd wear everybody out. Or if we were both like the Captain? We'd put everybody to sleep. The way we are now, we play off each other's personalities to create a good balance."

Toni and Daryl think that the only way to be successful is to be yourself, and to be positive about life. "I'm not a negative person," Toni says, "And I think it's kind of a waste of time feeling sorry for yourself. I understand getting blue every now and then 'cause I do too. But to allow yourself to wallow in it is a waste of time, and so I don't really like to contribute to that."

It's easy to see that the Captain and Tennille's positive way of looking at things has helped them considerably to become one of the most popular show business couples ever.

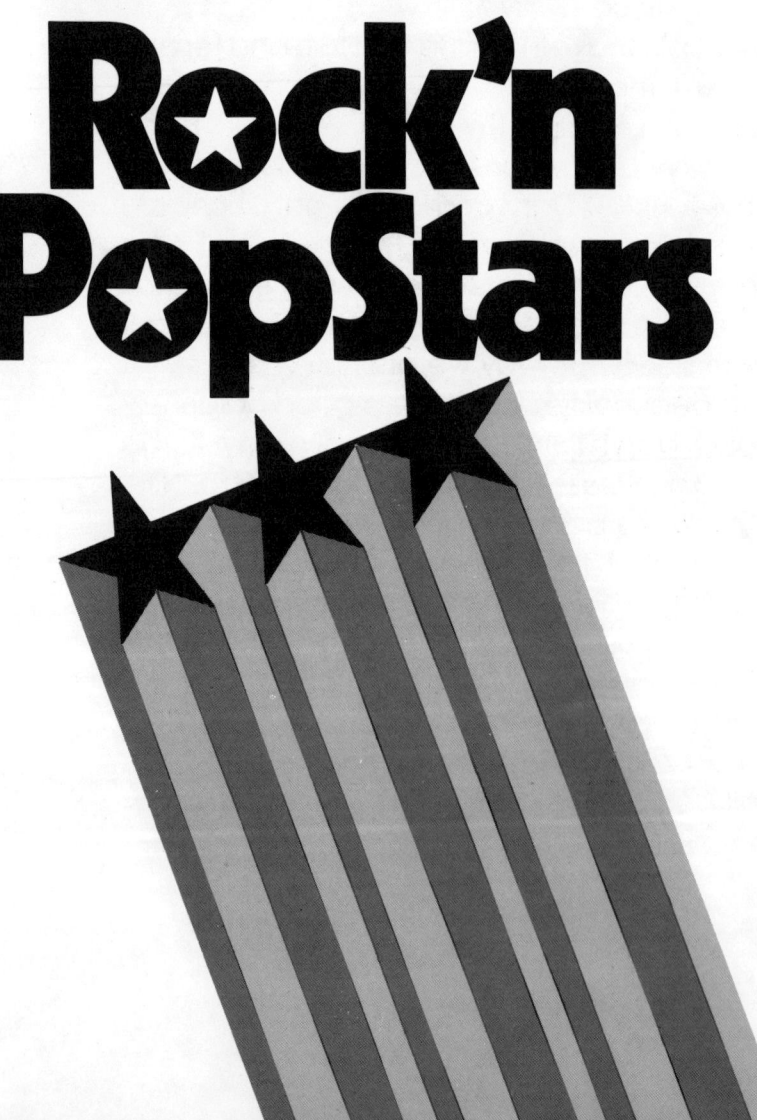

DIANA ROSS
THE OSMONDS
CHARLIE RICH
ELTON JOHN
CHICAGO
FRANK SINATRA
BARBRA STREISAND
OLIVIA NEWTON-JOHN
CAPTAIN AND TENNILLE
TONY ORLANDO
BARRY MANILOW
DONNY AND MARIE
SONNY AND CHER

JACKSON FIVE
CARLY SIMON
BOB DYLAN
JOHN DENVER
THE BEATLES
ELVIS PRESLEY
JOHNNY CASH
CHARLEY PRIDE
ARETHA FRANKLIN
ROBERTA FLACK
STEVIE WONDER
NEIL DIAMOND
CAROLE KING

Rock 'n Pop Stars